LUNCH AT 10 POMEGRANATE STREET

A collection of recipes to share

LUNCH AT
10 POMEGRANATE
STREET

A collection of recipes to share

Felicita Sala

SCRIBBLE

FOR MY MOTHER, WHOSE DOOR IS ALWAYS OPEN,
WHOSE TABLE IS ALWAYS FULL.

— F.S.

SOMETHING SMELLS GOOD
AT 10 POMEGRANATE STREET.
DELICIOUS, ACTUALLY!

IN THIS KITCHEN,
PILAR WHIZZES UP
TOMATOES IN A BIG POT.

1 KG RIPE TOMATOES

1-2 GARLIC CLOVES, MINCED

1 TSP SALT

200 g of YESTERDAY'S BREAD, CHOPPED

huile D'OLIVE EX

100 ml EXTRA VIRGIN OLIVE OIL

JAMÓN

2 HARD BOILED EGGS

SALMOREJO

CHOP THE TOMATOES AND BLEND IN A LARGE BOWL OR POT WITH THE MINCED GARLIC UNTIL SMOOTH. PASS THROUGH A SIEVE TO GET RID OF SEEDS. ADD THE BREAD AND BLEND UNTIL SMOOTH. MIX IN THE SALT AND OLIVE OIL. SERVE WITH CHOPPED HARD BOILED EGGS AND STRIPS OF JAMÓN SERRANO.

SERVES 6

NEXT DOOR, MISTER PING
STIR FRIES SOME BROCCOLI.
HIS NEPHEW BENJAMIN CALLS
THEM LITTLE TREES.

2 SMALL HEADS OF BROCCOLI, CHOPPED IN SMALL FLORETS

1 TBSP SESAME OIL + more for frying

SALT

1 TBSP SESAME SEEDS

1 TBSP MINCED GINGER

2 TBSP SOY SAUCE

Sesame oil 香油

SOY SAUCE

100 mL water or stock

LITTLE TREES
(SESAME SOY BROCCOLI)

TOAST SESAME SEEDS IN A HOT, DRY PAN UNTIL THEY START TO POP. IN A CUP, MAKE THE SAUCE BY MIXING SESAME OIL, SOY SAUCE AND WATER. HEAT UP A LARGE WOK, ADD A LITTLE SESAME OIL AND STIR FRY THE GINGER FOR 1 MINUTE AND THEN THE BROCCOLI ON HIGH HEAT FOR 2 MINUTES. ADD THE SAUCE AND STIR FRY FOR 5-6 MORE MINUTES. STIR IN THE SESAME SEEDS AND SEASON WITH SALT. SERVES 4

ACROSS THE HALL, MARIA MASHES
AVOCADOS WITH A FORK.

3 RIPE
AVOCADOS

1 FRESH RED CHILLI
OR A SMALL PIECE OF
RED PEPPER

A SMALL
BUNCH OF
CORIANDER

½ SMALL
RED
ONION

SALT
& PEPPER

OLIVE
OIL

3 or 4
CHERRY
TOMATOES

GUACAMOLE

MASH THE FLESH OF 3 AVOCADOS. FINELY CHOP THE TOMATOES, CHILLI,
RED ONION AND CORIANDER. ADD TO THE AVOCADOS ALONG WITH
THE LIME JUICE, A FEW DROPS OF OLIVE OIL, SALT AND PEPPER.
SERVE WITH NACHO CHIPS.

UPSTAIRS,
SEÑORA FLORES
SQUEEZES LIMES
INTO A POT OF BEANS.

2 GARLIC CLOVES, MINCED

1 TSP CRUSHED CUMIN

1 RED ONION

½ GREEN BELL PEPPER

JUICE OF 2 LIMES

BLACK BEANS

3 CANS OF BLACK BEANS (OR 750g COOKED + DRAINED)

1 TBSP TOMATO PASTE

1 TSP OREGANO

500 mL STOCK (OR BEAN-COOKING LIQUID)

4 STRIPS OF BACON, CHOPPED

BLACK BEAN SOUP

FINELY CHOP ONION AND BELL PEPPER. HEAT UP A LARGE POT, ADD SOME OLIVE OIL AND FRY BACON FOR 2 MINS, UNTIL BROWN. ADD ONION AND BELL PEPPER AND COOK ON GENTLE HEAT FOR 5 MINS. NOW ADD THE GARLIC, CUMIN, OREGANO AND TOMATO PASTE. STIR AND COOK ANOTHER MINUTE. ADD THE BEANS AND STOCK AND SEASON WITH SALT. SIMMER FOR ½ HOUR, STIRRING OCCASIONALLY. ADD LIME JUICE AT THE END AND SERVE WITH RICE AND SOME CORIANDER (OPTIONAL).   SERVES 4-6

MISTER MELVILLE THINKS
ABOUT THE BEST ANGLE
TO CUT INTO HIS FISH.

4 FILLETS OF LEMON SOLE
(OR OTHER WHITE FISH),
SKIN REMOVED

50g BUTTER

2 TBSP OLIVE OIL

LEMON JUICE

SALT & PEPPER

4 TBSP FLOUR

PARSLEY

A HANDFUL OF PINENUTS

SOLE MEUNIÈRE

TOSS THE FILLETS IN THE FLOUR AND SHAKE OFF EXCESS. HEAT
BUTTER AND OLIVE OIL IN A LARGE FRYING PAN. ADD FISH AND COOK
FOR 2 MINUTES UNTIL GOLDEN. TURN FISH AND SEASON WITH SALT
AND PEPPER. ADD PINENUTS AND COOK FOR ANOTHER 2 MINUTES.
ADD LEMON JUICE AND SOME CHOPPED PARSLEY, STIR THE PAN
A LITTLE AND SERVE.   SERVES 4

IN ANOTHER KITCHEN, SIGNORA LELLA
TASTES HER FAMOUS SAUCE, DECIDING
IT NEEDS MORE SALT.

500g SPAGHETTI

4 TBSP OLIVE OIL

2 SHALLOTS

BASIL

SALT

1 CLOVE OF GARLIC

PARMESAN

PASSATA di pomodo

700 g PASSATA

SPAGHETTI al POMODORO

IN A POT, HEAT OLIVE OIL AND GENTLY COOK THE FINELY DICED SHALLOTS AND THE WHOLE GARLIC CLOVE FOR 3-4 MINUTES. ADD THE PASSATA AND TURN UP THE HEAT FOR 2 MINUTES. ADD ½ CUP OF WATER AND SOME SALT, COVER THE POT AND COOK ON VERY LOW HEAT FOR AT LEAST 1 HOUR, STIRRING OCCASIONALLY. ADD SOME BASIL LEAVES IN THE LAST 10 MINUTES. WHEN THE SAUCE IS ALMOST DONE, ADD THE SPAGHETTI TO A LARGE POT OF BOILING, SALTED WATER. WHEN COOKED, DRAIN THE SPAGHETTI AND ADD TO THE POT OF SAUCE, STIRRING ON HIGH HEAT FOR 1 MINUTE. SERVE WITH GRATED PARMESAN AND SOME BASIL LEAVES.   SERVES 4-5

UP ON THE THIRD FLOOR, MISTER SINGH OPENS A CAN OF COCONUT MILK.

2 CUPS / 400g RED SPLIT LENTILS

1 TSP TURMERIC

2 TBSP CURRY POWDER

3 TBSP COCONUT OIL OR GHEE

1 CAN OF COCONUT MILK

1L / 4 CUPS WATER

1 TBSP GRATED GINGER

2 CARROTS

1 CLOVE OF GARLIC, MINCED

3 TBSP TOMATO PASTE

2 TSP SALT

4 GREEN ONIONS

COCONUT DAHL

FINELY CHOP THE CARROTS AND GREEN ONIONS. GENTLY COOK THE VEGETABLES IN A LARGE POT WITH THE OIL/GHEE AND A PINCH OF SALT. ADD THE GINGER, GARLIC, TURMERIC AND CURRY POWDER. STIR FOR 1 MINUTE, THEN ADD THE TOMATO PASTE WITH A LITTLE WATER AND STIR SOME MORE. ADD THE LENTILS AND WATER AND SIMMER FOR 20 MINUTES. ADD THE COCONUT MILK AND SALT AND SIMMER FOR ANOTHER 15 MINUTES, STIRRING OCCASIONALLY AND ADDING A LITTLE WATER IF NEEDED. SERVE WITH RICE. SERVES 6-8.

MEANWHILE,
MRS GREENPEA DELIGHTS
IN THE GOLDEN CRUST
OF HER MINI-QUICHES.

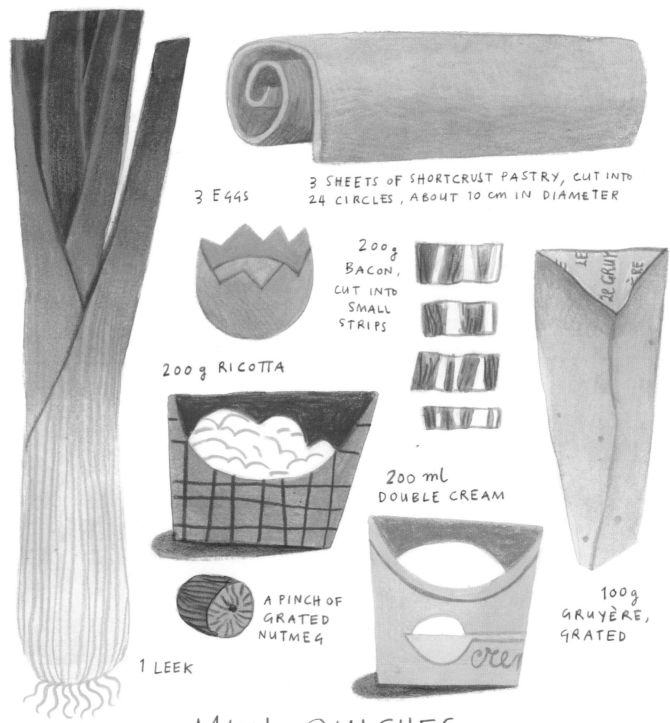

3 EGGS

3 SHEETS OF SHORTCRUST PASTRY, CUT INTO 24 CIRCLES, ABOUT 10 cm IN DIAMETER

200g BACON, CUT INTO SMALL STRIPS

200g RICOTTA

200 ml DOUBLE CREAM

100g GRUYÈRE, GRATED

A PINCH OF GRATED NUTMEG

1 LEEK

MINI-QUICHES

PREHEAT OVEN TO 180°C. REMOVE TOUGH DARK LEAVES FROM THE LEEK, CUT IT IN HALF LENGTHWISE AND RINSE WELL. CUT LEEK INTO THIN SLICES AND COOK IN A PAN ON GENTLE HEAT WITH A LITTLE BUTTER AND A PINCH OF SALT FOR 20 MINUTES UNTIL SOFT. FRY BACON FOR A FEW MINUTES UNTIL CRISPY. IN A LARGE BOWL, COMBINE THE RICOTTA, CREAM, EGGS AND CHEESE WITH A PINCH OF SALT AND SOME NUTMEG. MIX IN THE LEEK AND BACON ONCE THEY ARE COOL. PLACE 12 PASTRY CIRCLES IN A 12-CUP MUFFIN TRAY AND FILL WITH 2-3 TEASPOONS OF THE MIX. BAKE FOR 15-20 MINUTES AND REPEAT WITH THE SECOND BATCH. MAKES 24.

JOSEF AND RAFIK TAKE THE JOB
OF ROLLING VERY SERIOUSLY.

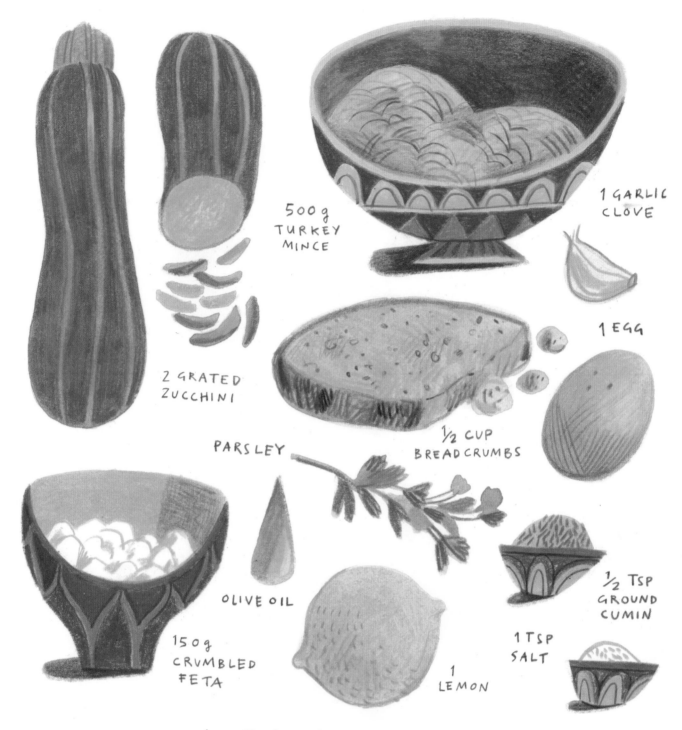

500g
TURKEY
MINCE

1 GARLIC
CLOVE

1 EGG

2 GRATED
ZUCCHINI

½ CUP
BREADCRUMBS

PARSLEY

OLIVE OIL

150g
CRUMBLED
FETA

1 LEMON

1 TSP
SALT

½ TSP
GROUND
CUMIN

MEATBALLS
(with turkey, zucchini & feta)

PREHEAT OVEN TO 200°C. IN A PAN, COOK THE ZUCCHINI WITH A LITTLE OIL AND A
PINCH OF SALT UNTIL SOFT. SOFTEN THE BREAD CRUMBS WITH MILK OR WATER AND
SQUEEZE OUT EXCESS LIQUID. MINCE THE GARLIC AND FINELY CHOP THE PARSLEY.
PLACE THE MINCE IN A LARGE BOWL AND ADD THE ZUCCHINI, BREAD, GARLIC, PARSLEY,
CUMIN, SALT, EGG, FETA, AND THE ZEST OF 1 LEMON. MIX WELL WITH YOUR HANDS,
THEN MAKE SPOON-SIZED BALLS. HEAT UP A LARGE PAN AND FRY THE MEATBALLS
WITH SOME OLIVE OIL UNTIL GOLDEN BROWN (5 MINUTES). PLACE IN A ROASTING
TRAY LINED WITH OVEN PAPER AND BAKE FOR 6-7 MINUTES UNTIL COOKED.
SERVE WITH A LITTLE LEMON JUICE.

MISS ISHIDA
QUIETLY REACHES
FOR A BOTTLE OF MIRIN.

2 BONELESS, SKINLESS CHICKEN THIGHS

3 TBSP SOY SAUCE

3 TBSP MIRIN

MIRIN みりん

S

100 ml DASHI OR CHICKEN STOCK

3 SHALLOTS

2 EGGS

2 TBSP SUGAR

2 CUPS COOKED RICE

1 GREEN ONION

OYAKO DON
(chicken & egg rice)

IN A BOWL, MIX TOGETHER THE STOCK, MIRIN, SOY SAUCE AND SUGAR. THINLY SLICE THE SHALLOTS AND CUT CHICKEN IN BITE-SIZED PIECES. PLACE SHALLOTS AND STOCK MIX IN A SMALL PAN AND BRING TO A BOIL. ADD CHICKEN, LOWER HEAT TO MEDIUM-LOW AND COOK FOR 6 MINUTES. LIGHTLY BEAT THE EGGS AND POUR OVER THE CHICKEN, STIRRING GENTLY FOR 30 SECONDS. TURN OFF THE HEAT, COVER AND LEAVE TO REST FOR A COUPLE OF MINUTES, SERVE OVER FLUFFY RICE WITH SOME SLICED GREEN ONIONS ON TOP (OPTIONAL). MAKE THIS DISH IN SMALL BATCHES OF 1 OR 2. SERVES 2

IN ANOTHER APARTMENT,
MISTER IBRAHIM
REMEMBERS HIS CHILDHOOD
HOME AND SMILES.

3 MEDIUM-LONG EGGPLANTS

2 CLOVES of GARLIC, MINCED.

3 TBSP OLIVE OIL

1/2 TSP SALT

CHOPPED PARSLEY

TAHINI

3 TBSP TAHINI

1/2 TSP SMOKED PAPRIKA

3 TBSP LEMON JUICE

BABA GANOUSH

PREHEAT OVEN GRILL TO 200°C. ROAST WHOLE EGGPLANTS ON A BAKING TRAY FOR 1 HOUR, UNTIL SOFT INSIDE. WHEN THEY ARE COOL, SCOOP OUT THE FLESH INTO A BOWL. SQUASH WITH A FORK OR PUREE WITH AN IMMERSION BLENDER. MIX IN TAHINI, MINCED GARLIC, LEMON JUICE, PAPRIKA, SALT, PARSLEY AND OLIVE OIL. BLEND UNTIL SMOOTH. SERVE WITH PITA BREAD OR CARROT STICKS.

AS THEY REACH FOR YET ANOTHER
OLIVE, PENELOPE AND MILES
BELIEVE IT IS THEY WHO ARE
DOING THE COOKING.

200g (1 CUP) WHITE RICE

1 KG SPINACH

250ml (1 CUP) WATER

JUICE OF HALF A LEMON

2 RED ONIONS

1 CUP PITTED GREEK OLIVES

Kalamata OLIVES

3 GARLIC CLOVES

150 g FETA

GREEN RICE

FINELY CHOP ONIONS AND SAUTÉ IN A LARGE POT WITH OLIVE OIL AND A PINCH OF SALT UNTIL GOLDEN (ABOUT 10 MINS). MINCE THE GARLIC AND ADD TO THE POT ALONG WITH THE RICE AND TOAST FOR 1 MINUTE. ADD SPINACH IN PARTS UNTIL ALL IS WILTED. ADD WATER AND 1 TEASPOON OF SALT, COVER AND COOK ON LOW HEAT FOR 15 MINUTES. IF NECESSARY, ADD WATER TOWARDS THE END AND STIR. WHEN RICE IS COOKED, ADD CRUMBLED FETA, CHOPPED OLIVES AND LEMON JUICE.

SERVES 4-6

UP ON THE FIFTH FLOOR, JEREMIAH CANNOT SEEM TO REMEMBER THE WORDS TO HIS FAVOURITE SONG.

100g SOFTENED BUTTER

½ TSP SALT

½ TSP BICARB

1 TSP VANILLA

100g CHOCOLATE

100g CRUNCHY PEANUT BUTTER

170g FLOUR

1 EGG

125g BROWN SUGAR

PEANUT BUTTER & CHOC CHIP COOKIES

BEAT TOGETHER THE BUTTER, PEANUT BUTTER AND VANILLA UNTIL FLUFFY. BEAT IN THE EGG. ADD SUGAR, FLOUR, SALT + BICARB. CHOP THE CHOCOLATE INTO SMALL CHIPS AND ADD TO THE MIX. WITH YOUR HANDS, MIX THE DOUGH ON A LIGHTLY FLOURED SURFACE. ROLL DOUGH INTO A LOG SHAPE, ABOUT 5 CM IN DIAMETER. WRAP IN CLING FILM AND REFRIGERATE FOR 2 HOURS. PREHEAT OVEN TO 180°C. CUT THE LOG INTO 1 CM ROUNDS AND BAKE ON A TRAY FOR 15 MINUTES UNTIL GOLDEN BUT STILL SOFT.

JEMIMA AND ROSIE ARGUE
OVER WHO TOOK THE LAST
BANANA.

2 OR 3 RIPE BANANAS

150g
3/4 CUP BROWN SUGAR

125g BUTTER

VANILLA

2 TSP BAKING POWDER
+
1/2 TSP SALT

2 EGGS

1 CUP (150g) BLUEBERRIES

150g YOGHURT

200g FLOUR
(1 1/2 CUPS)

BANANA & BLUEBERRY BREAD

PREHEAT OVEN TO 180°C. BUTTER AND FLOUR A LOAF TIN. IN A BOWL, MIX BUTTER, EGGS AND SUGAR. ADD BANANAS AND MASH WITH A FORK. ADD YOGHURT. ADD FLOUR WITH BAKING POWDER AND SALT, AND MIX WELL. LIGHTLY COAT THE BLUEBERRIES IN FLOUR AND GENTLY FOLD THEM INTO THE MIX. POUR BATTER IN THE LOAF TIN AND BAKE 45-50 MINUTES.

SMELLING THE FIRST
STRAWBERRIES OF THE YEAR,
MATILDA DREAMS ABOUT
THE SUMMER THAT WILL COME.

3 PUNNETS OF STRAWBERRIES (700g)

1 TBSP LEMON JUICE

200g FLOUR

CRÈME FRAÎCHE TO SERVE

½ CUP/ 50g SLIVERED ALMONDS

80g SUGAR

100g BUTTER

STRAWBERRY CRUMBLE

PREHEAT OVEN TO 180°C. CUT STRAWBERRIES IN HALF AND PLACE IN A SMALL OVEN TIN WITH LEMON JUICE AND A SPOONFUL OF SUGAR. CUT BUTTER INTO SMALL CUBES AND MIX WITH FLOUR AND SUGAR IN A BOWL. RUB THE MIXTURE WITH YOUR FINGERS UNTIL YOU HAVE A CRUMBLY MIX, LIKE WET SAND. COVER STRAWBERRIES WITH THE CRUMBLE AND PAT DOWN. SPRINKLE ALMONDS ON TOP. BAKE 40 MINUTES UNTIL GOLDEN. SERVE WARM WITH CRÈME FRAÎCHE OR VANILLA ICE CREAM.

EVERYTHING IS READY.
IT'S TIME TO GO
DOWNSTAIRS.

PULL UP A CHAIR AND GRAB A PLATE! EVERYBODY'S WELCOME AT 10 POMEGRANATE STREET.

THE ILLUSTRATIONS IN THIS BOOK ARE MADE WITH WATERCOLOURS AND COLOURED PENCILS.

Published by Scribble, an imprint of Scribe Publications, 2019

18–20 Edward Street, Brunswick, Victoria 3056, Australia

2 John Street, Clerkenwell, London, WC1N 2ES, United Kingdom

Text and illustrations © Felicita Sala 2018

Originally published in French as *Au 10 Rue des Jardins* by Editions Cambourakis, 2018
Translation © 2018, Scribble, an imprint of Scribe Publications
This edition was published by arrangement with The Picture Book Agency, France
All rights reserved.

Printed in China by Everbest Printing Investment Limited

9781925849059 (Australian hardback)
9781911617983 (UK hardback)
9781912854158 (UK paperback)

CiP records for this title are available from the National Library of Australia
and the British Library

scribblekidsbooks.com
scribepublications.com.au
scribepublications.co.uk